D

An Introduction to Internet of Things(IoT)

Sureshkumar Sundaram
Devi kala Rathinam Duraisamy
SriVaishnavi Dharmaraj

An Introduction to Internet of Things(IoT)

A Simple Way of Learning IoT

LAP LAMBERT Academic Publishing

Cover image: www.ingimage.com

Publisher:
LAP LAMBERT Academic Publishing
is a trademark of
International Book Market Service Ltd., member of OmniScriptum Publishing Group
17 Meldrum Street, Beau Bassin 71504, Mauritius

Printed at: see last page
ISBN: 978-613-9-58750-6

INTRODUCTION TO INTERNET OF THINGS (IoT)

Internet of Things (IoT) comprises things that have unique identities with many connecting devices, machines and tools to the internet by means of wireless technologies. Nearly 9 billion 'Things' connected to the Internet but in future nearly 20 billion things will be connected. The IoT enabling technologies such as Wireless Sensor Network (WSN), Big-Data Analytics, low-power embedded systems, cloud computing, machine learning, and networking.

Definition of IoT

A dynamic global network infrastructure with self-configuring capabilities based on standard and interoperable communication protocols where physical and virtual "things" have identities, physical attributes and virtual personalities and use intelligent interfaces, and are seamlessly integrated into the information network, often communicate data associated with users and their environment.

Characteristics of IoT

- Dynamic and Self-Adapting
- Self-Configuring
- Interoperable Communication Protocols
- Unique Identity
- Integrated into the Information Network

Evolution of Connected Devices

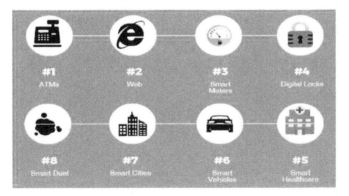

- ATM

These universal money dispensers went online for the first time way back in 1974.

- WEB

World Wide Web made its debut in 1991 to revolutionize computing and communications.

- SMART METERS

The first power meters to communicate remotely with the grid were installed in the early 2000s.

- DIGITAL LOCKS

Smartphones can be used to lock and unlock doors remotely, and business owners can change key codes rapidly to grant or restrict access to employees and guests.

- SMART HEALTHCARE

Devices connect to hospitals, doctors and relatives to alert them of medical emergencies and take preventive measures.

- SMART VEHICLES

Vehicles self-diagnose themselves and alert owners about system failures.

- SMART CITIES

City-wide infrastructure communicating amongst themselves for unified and synchronized operations and information dissemination.

- SMART DUST

Computers smaller than a grain of sand can be sprayed or injected almost anywhere to measure chemicals in the soil or to diagnose problems in the human body.

Modern Day IoT Applications

- ✓ Smart Parking
- ✓ Noise Urban Maps
- ✓ Smart Lighting
- ✓ Waste Management
- ✓ Smart Grid
- ✓ Tank level
- ✓ Photovoltaic Installations
- ✓ Silos Stock Calculation
- ✓ Landslide and Avalanche Prevention
- ✓ Radiation Levels
- ✓ Snow Level Monitoring
- ✓ Supply Chain Control
- ✓ Smart Product Management
- ✓ Intelligent Shopping Applications
- ✓ Traffic Congestion
- ✓ Smartphone Detection
- ✓ Smart Roads
- ✓ Water Flow
- ✓ Structural health
- ✓ River Floods
- ✓ Liquid Presence
- ✓ Air Pollution
- ✓ Forest Fire Detection
- ✓ Earthquake Early Detection
- ✓ Water Leakages
- ✓ Explosive and Hazardous Gases
- ✓ NFC Payment
- ✓ Perimeter Access Control

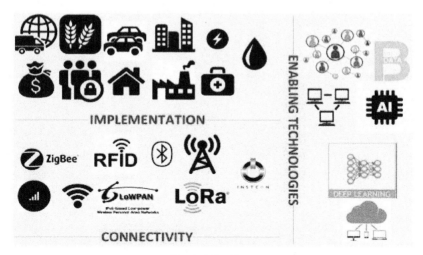

Fig: IoT Enablers

Baseline Technologies

The following are the technologies that are very closely related to IoT include

- Machine-to-Machine (M2M) communications
- Cyber-Physical-Systems (CPS)
- Web-of-Things (WoT)

IoT vs. Machine-to-Machine (M2M) communications

Machine-to-Machine (M2M)refers to communications and interactions between various machines and devices. Such interactions can occur via a cloud computing infrastructure. M2M offers for managing devices and devices interaction, while also collecting machine and/or sensor data. M2M is a term introduced by telecommunication services providers and, pays emphasis on machines interactions via one or more telecommunication networks (e.g., 3G, 4G, 5G, satellite, public networks).

M2M is part of the IoT, while M2M standards have a prominent place in the IoT standards landscape. However, IoT has a broader scope than M2M, since it comprises a broader range of interactions, including interactions between devices/things, things and people, things with applications and people with applications. It also enables the composition of workflows comprising all of the above interactions. IoT includes the notion of internet connectivity, but is not necessarily focused on the use of telecommunication networks.

IoT vs. Cyber-Physical-Systems (CPS)

Cyber-Physical-Systems (CPS) used to represent the next generation embedded intelligent ICT systems. It is interconnected, collaborative, interdependent, autonomous and provide computing and communication, monitoring of physical components and process in various applications. The CPS need scalable, distributed, decentralized in future whichallow to interact with human, environment and machines which is being connected to internet. Some features like Adaptability, reactivity, security and optimality are embedded in the system.

IoT vs. Web-of-Things (WoT)

From a developer's side, the **Web-of-Things (WoT)**enables access and control over IoT resources and applications by using mainstream web technologies like HTML 5.0, JavaScript, Ajax, PHP, Ruby n' Rails etc. The RESTful principles and REST APIs is used to build WoT, which enable both developers and deployers to benefit from the popularity and maturity of web technologies. Still now various challenges like scalability, security etc are faced in building the WoT. IoT is about creating a network of objects, people, things, systems and applications, WoT tries to integrate them to the Web. Technically speaking, WoT can be thought as a flavor/option of an application layer added over the IoT's network layer. However, the scope of IoT applications is broader and includes systems that are not accessible through the web.

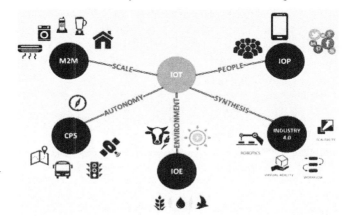

Fig: Terminological Interdependence

6LoWPAN

- 6LoWPANstands for**Low-power Wireless Personal Area Networks over IPv6**.
- Allows for the smallest devices with limited processing ability to transmit information wirelessly using an Internet protocol.
- It allows low-power devices to connect with the Internet.
- It is created by the Internet Engineering Task Force (IETF) -RFC 5933 and RFC 4919.

Features of 6LoWPANs

4

- Allows IEEE 802.15.4 radios to carry 128bit addresses of Internet Protocol version 6(IPv6).
- Header compression and address translation techniques allow the IEEE 802.15.4 radios to access the Internet.
- IPv6 packets compressed and reformatted to fit the IEEE 802.15.4 packet format.
- Uses include IoT, Smart grid, and M2M applications.

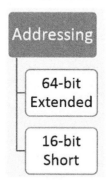

Fig: 6LoWPANs Addressing

64-bit addresses: Globally unique
16 bit addresses: which is PAN specific and also assigned by PAN coordinator
IPv6 multicast is not supported by 802.15.4
IPv6 packets are carried as link layer broadcast frames.

RFID

- RFID stands for **Radio-Frequency Identification**.
- The data's are digitally encoded in RFID tags, which can be read by a reader.
- RFID is somewhat similar to barcodes.
- The data read from tags are stored in a database by the reader.
- As compared to traditional barcodes and QR codes, RFID tag data can be read outside the line-of-sight.

RFID Features
- The RFID tag consists of an integrated circuit and an antenna.
- The tag is covered by a protective material which act as a shield against environmental factors like rainfall, wind etc.
- Tags may be passive or active.
- Passive RFID tags are the most widely used.
- Passive tags have to be powered by a reader inductively before they can transmit information, but the active tag have their own power supply.

Working Principle
- It is derived from Automatic Identification and Data Capture (AIDC) technology.

- AIDC uses wired communication for object identification, data collection and mapping of collected data to computer systems with little or no human intervention.
- AIDC functions can be performed using radio waves in RFID.
- The main components of RFID system includes an RFID reader, RFID tag or smart label and antenna.

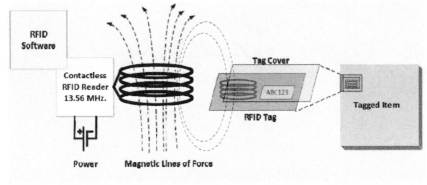

Fig: RFID working

Applications of RFID
The following are the applications of RFID. They are
- Inventory management
- Personnel tracking
- Asset tracking
- ID badging
- Controlling access to restricted areas
- Supply chain management
- Counterfeit prevention (e.g. in the pharmaceutical industry)

MQTT
- MQTT stands for **Message Queue Telemetry Transport**.
- ISO standard (ISO/IEC PRF 20922).
- MQTT was introduced by IBM in 1999 and standardized by OASIS in 2013.
- It is publish-subscribe based lightweight messaging protocol for use in conjunction with the TCP/IP protocol.
- It is designed to provide connectivity between applications and middle wares on one side and networks and communications on the other side.

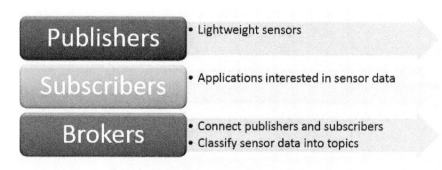

Fig: MQTT Components

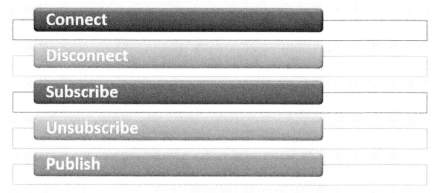

Fig: MQTT Methods

Applications of MQTT
- Facebook Messenger
- Amazon Web Services
- Microsoft Azure
- EVRYTHNG IoTplatform
- Adafruit

CoAP
- CoAP stands for **Constrained Application Protocol**.
- Web transfer protocol for use with constrained nodes and networks.
- It is mainly designed for Machine to Machine (M2M) applications.
- CoAP is based on Request-Response model between end-points.
- The Client-Server interaction is asynchronous over the User Datagram Protocol (UDP).

7

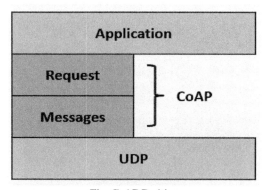

Fig: CoAP Position

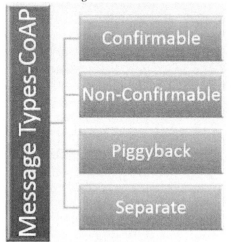

Fig: CoAPMessage Types

Features of CoAP
- CoAP used to reduced overheads and parsing complexity.
- It is URL and content-type support.
- Support for the discovery of resources provided by known CoAPservices.
- Simple subscription for a resource, and resulting push notifications.
- Simple caching based on maximum message age.

XMPP
- XMPP stands for **Extensible Messaging and Presence Protocol**.
- The message oriented middleware is based on XML (Extensible Markup Language) which is a communication protocol.

8

- It is real-time data exchange and open standard protocol.
- XMPP uses a client-server architecture.
- It is decentralized, no central server is required.
- XMPP provides for the discovery of services residing locally or across a network and there is an information availability.

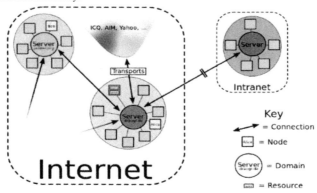

Fig: XMPP

Applications of XMPP
- Publish-subscribe systems
- Video
- Signaling for VoIP
- Gaming
- File transfer
- Internet of Things applications
- Social networking services
- Smart grid

AMQP
- AMQP stands for **Advanced Message Queuing Protocol**.
- ISO standard: ISO/IEC 19464
- Open standard for passing business messages between applications or organizations.
- Connects between systems and business processes.
- It is a binary application layer protocol.
- Basic unit of data is a frame.
- ISO standard: ISO/IEC 19464

Exchange	• Part of Broker • Receives messages and routes them to Queues
Queue	• Separate queues for separate business processes • Consumers receive messages from queues
Bindings	• Rules for distributing messages (who can access what message, destination of the message)

Fig: Components of AMQP

Features of AMQP

- Security
- Interoperability
- Reliability
- Routing
- Open standard
- Queuing

Applications of AMQP

- Monitoring and global update sharing.
- The different systems can be connected and processes to talk to each other.
- AMQP makes the server to respond immediately and delegate time consuming tasks for later processing.
- The offline client can fetch the data with less time.
- Distributing a message to multiple recipients for consumption.
- It is fully asynchronous functionality for systems.
- The reliability can be increased and uptime of application deployments.

Communication Protocols of IoT

The following are the communication protocols of IoTs:

- IEEE 802.15.4
- 6LoWPAN
- Zigbee
- Wireless HART
- ISA 100
- Z-Wave
- NFC
- Bluetooth
- RFID

IEEE 802.15.4

- IEEE 802.15.4standard for low data-rate WPAN.
- It is developed for low data rate monitoring and control applications.
- It is low power consumption.
- Operates in the ISM band.
- It uses only first two layers (PHY, MAC) and the logical link control (LLC) and the service convergence the sub-layer (SSCS) additions to communicate with all upper layers.

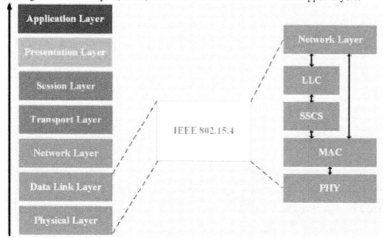

Fig: IEEE 802.15.4

ZigBee

- ZigBeeismost widely deployed enhancement of IEEE 802.15.4.
- It is defined by layer 3 and above but it works with the 802.15.4 layers 1 and 2.
- The standard uses layers 3 and 4 to define additional communication enhancements.
- ZigBeeis used mainly in wireless sensor networks using the mesh topology.

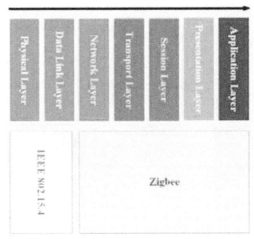

Fig: ZigBee

ZDO
- ZigBee Device Object
  (Device management, Security, Policies)

APS
- Application Support Sub-layer
  (Interfacing and control services, bridge
  between network and other layers)

Fig: Important Components

Applications of ZigBee

- Building automation
- Remote control
- Smart energy
- Home automation
- Health care
- Telecom services
- Light Link for control of LED lighting

HART & Wireless HART

- HART stands for Highway Addressable Remote Transducer(HART) Protocol.
- It is mainly developed for networked smart field devices.
- It is a wireless protocol which makes the implementation of HART cheaper and easier.

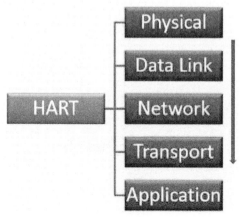

Fig: HART

NFC

- NFC stands for Near Field Communication.
- It is mainly designed for use by devices within close proximity to each other.
- All type of NFCs are similar but communicate in slightly different ways.
- FeliCais most commonly found in Japan.

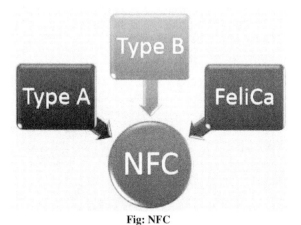

Fig: NFC

Types of NFC

There are two types of NFCs-

- Passive NFC
- Active NFC

13

Passive NFC
- The passive NFC device contain information which can be read by other device.
- Eg: Supermarket products.

Active NFC
- The active NFC device is used to collect as well as transmit the information.
- Eg: Smart phone

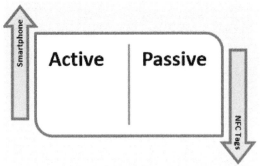

Fig: Types of NFC

NFC Applications
- Parcel tracking
- Smartphone based payments
- Information tags in posters and advertisements
- Low-power home automation systems
- Computer game synchronized toys

Bluetooth
- It is a wireless short range communications technology.
- It is portable unit and it maintains high levels of security.
- It is based on Ad-hoc technology also known as Ad-hoc Pico nets.

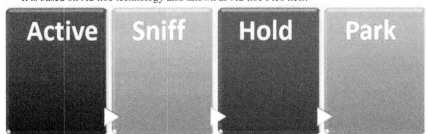

Fig: Bluetooth Modes

Active-Actively transmitting or receiving data
Sniff-Sleeps and only listens for transmissions at a set interval

14

Hold-Power saving mode where a device sleeps for a defined periods and then returns back to active mode.

Park-Slave will become inactive until the master tells it to wake back up.

Applications of Bluetooth

- Home automation
- Audio players
- Smartphones
- Hands free headphones
- Toys
- Sensor networks

Z-wave

- Z-wave is a protocol used for communication among devices.
- It uses RF for signaling and control.
- Operating frequency in US is 908.42 MHz & in Europe 868.42 MHz.
- The main mode of operation is mesh network topology and it can support up to 232 nodes in a network.

Wireless Sensor Networks (WSNs)

- WSN consist of large number of sensor nodes.
- Those sensors are deployed over the area.
- The sensor nodes are used to collaborate with one another and used to measure itssurroundingenvironment. (Eg: sound, temperature, humidity, distance etc.)
- The measurement are then transformedintodigitalsignalsandprocessed torevealsomepropertiesofthephenomenaaroundsensors.
- There are many intermediate nodes which can act as relaynodestotransmitdatatowardsthesink nodeusingamulti-hoppath.

Applications of WSN

- Temperature measurement
- Lighting condition
- Humidity level
- Air pressure
- Soil makeup
- Vibration
- Noise level
- Agriculture

a) Soil sensor node   b) Temperature Flux sensor node   c) Weather sensor node

Fig: Example of Wireless Sensor

Challenges
- Scalability
- Quality of service
- Energy efficiency
- Security

Applications of WSNs
- Fire Monitoring
- Healthcare
- Home automation
- Parking system
- Street light monitoring
- Smart dustbin
- Agriculture

Coverage Problems in Static WSNs
There are three coverage problem in static WSNs
- Area coverage
- Point coverage
- Barrier coverage

Mobile Wireless Sensor Networks
- MWSN is Mobile Ad hoc Network (MANET)
- MANET is Infrastructure less network

It follow the following self-CHOPproperties
- o Self-Configure
- o Self-Heal
- o Self-Optimize
- o Self-Protect

Underwater MWSNs
It used to senses different parameters under the sea or water levels.
It can be linked with **Autonomous Underwater Vehicles (AUVs)**.
Applications of Underwater MWSNs

16

- Monitoring-marine life
- Water quality

Terrestrial MWSNs

The Terrestrial MWSNssensor nodes typically deployed over land surface.
It can be linked with **Unmanned Aerial Vehicles (UAVs).**

Applications of Terrestrial MWSNs

- Wildlife monitoring
- Surveillance
- Object tracking

Aerial MWSNs

- InAerial MWSNs nodes fly on the air and sense the data.
- Example of Aerial MWSNs is **Unmanned Aerial Vehicles (UAVs)**

Applications of Aerial MWSNs

- Surveillance
- Multimedia data gathering

UAV Networks

- UAV is Mesh or Star networks.
- It is more Flexible and manageable of new services using SDN.
- The routing protocol should be adaptive in nature.
- It is contribute towards greening of the network.
- It is Multi-tasking and has large coverage area.
- UAV is easily reconfigurable for varying missions.

Considerations in UAV Networks

- Speed of Mission
- Antenna
- Failure to coordinate
- Complexity of Control
- Survivability
- Failures
- Bandwidth required
- Cost
- Scalability

UAV Network Constraints

- Prone to malfunction
- Physically prone to environmental effects: winds, rain, etc.
- Frequent link breakages
- Very complex
- Huge power requirements

UAV Network Advantages

- High Survivability
- High Reliability

- Single Malfunction Proof
- Efficient
- Cost Effective
- Speeded up missions

Machine to Machine Communication (M2M)

- M2M is a communication between machines or device with computing and also with some communication facilities.
- It is free of human intervention.
- M2M is similar to industrial supervisory control and also data acquisition systems (SCADA).
- SCADA is designed for isolated systems using proprietary solutions.

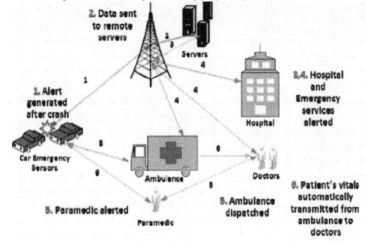

Fig: M2M communication

Applications of M2M

- Civil protection and public safety
- Environmental monitoring
- Supply Chain Management (SCM)
- Intelligent Transport Systems (ITSs)
- Energy & utility distribution industry (smart grid)
- Healthcare
- Military applications
- Automation of building
- Agriculture
- Home networks

Features of M2M

- Low cost
- Large number of nodes or devices
- Energy efficient
- Small traffic per machine/device
- Large quantity of collective data
- M2M communication free from human intervention.
- Human intervention required for operational stability and sustainability

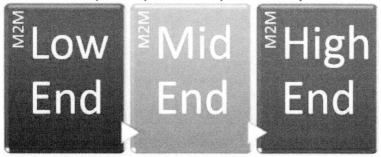

Fig: M2M Node Types

Low-end Sensor Nodes

- Low-end Sensor Nodes are cheap, and have low capabilities.
- It is static, energy efficient and simple.
- Deployment has high density in order to increase network lifetime and survivability.
- Resource constrained, and no IP support.
  Basic functionalities such as, data aggregation, auto configuration, and power saving.
- It is mainly used for environment monitoring applications.

Mid-end Sensor Nodes

- Mid-end Sensor Nodes is more expensive than low-end sensor nodes.
- Nodes may have mobility.
- There are few constraints with respect to complexity and energy efficiency.
- There are some additional functionalities are available
  - Localization
  - Quality of Service (QoS) support
  - TCP/IP support
  - Power control or traffic control
  - Intelligence

Applications

- Home networks
- Asset management
- SCM

- Industrial automation

High-end Sensor Nodes

Low density deployment.

Able to handle multimedia data (video) with QoS requirements.

Mobility is essential.

Example: smartphones.

Application

- ITS and military
- Bio/medical applications

Current Challenges in IoT

- Large Scale of Co-Operation
- Global Heterogeneity
- Unknown IoT Device Configuration
- Semantic Conflicts

Interoperability

Interoperability is a characteristic of a product or system, whose interfaces are completely understood, to work with other products or systems, present or future, in either implementationoraccess,withoutanyrestrictions.

- Communicate meaningfully
- Exchange data or services

Different Types of Interoperability?

- **User Interoperability**

User Interoperability defines the problem between a user and a device

- **Device Interoperability**

Device Interoperability defines the problem between two different devices

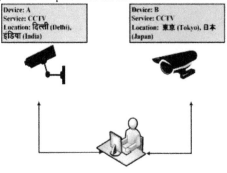

American User U

Fig: Example of Device and User Interoperability

Arduino

- Arduino is an open source based electronic programmable board (micro controller) and software(IDE).

20

- It used to accepts analog and digital signals as input and gives desired output.
- There is no extra hardware's are required to load a program into the controller board.

Types of Arduino Board
- ATMEGA328 microcontroller
- ATMEGA32u4 microcontroller
- ATMEGA2560 microcontroller
- AT91SAM3X8E microcontroller

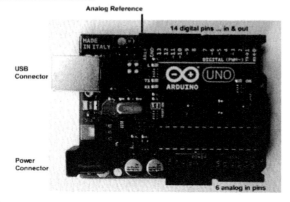

Board Details
- Power Supply: USB or power barrel jack
- Voltage Regulator
- Tx-Rx LED Indicator
- LED Power Indicator
- Output power, Ground
- Analog Input Pins
- Digital I/O Pins

ArduinoIDE
- It is an open source software that is used to program the Arduino controller board.
- There is a variations of the C and C++ programming language.
- It can be downloaded from Arduino'sofficial websiteand installed into PC.

Set Up
- The board can be powered by connecting it to a PC through USB cable
- ArduinoIDE is launched.
- The board type is set and also the port for the board is set.
- TOOLS -> BOARD -> select your board.
- TOOLS -> PORT -> select your port.

Fig: Setup

ArduinoIDE Overview

- The process of coding the program in Arduino IDE is called a SKETCH.

Fig:ArduinoIDE Overview

- To create a new sketch
    File -> New
- To open an existing sketch
    File -> open ->
- There are some basic ready-to-use sketches available in the EXAMPLES section
    File -> Examples -> select any program

22

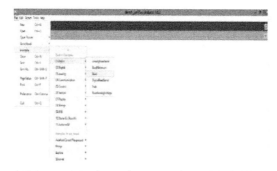

- Verify
  Checks the code for compilation errors.
- Upload
  Uploads the final code to the controller board.
- New
  Creates a new blank sketch with basic structure.
- Open
  Opens an existing sketch.
- Save
  Saves the current sketch.

- Serial Monitor
  The serial console gets open
- The printed data to the console gets displayed here.

Sketch Structure

There are two parts in Sketch:
  o Setup ()
  o Loop ()

- The code starts at the function point Setup(), it is just like the main() function in C and C++.
- In Setup() function I/O Variables, pin modes are initialized.
- Loop() function used for iterates the specific task in the program.

23

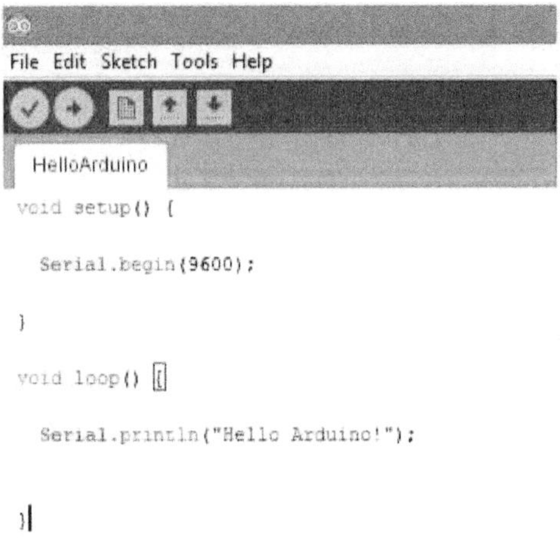

File Edit Sketch Tools Help
HelloArduino
void setup() {
Serial.begin(9600);
}
void loop() {
Serial.println("Hello Arduino!");
}

Fig: Sketch Structure

Supported Datatype

The following data types are supported by Arduino

- Void
- Long
- Int
- Char
- Boolean
- Unsigned char
- Byte
- Unsigned int
- Word
- Unsigned long
- Float
- Double
- Array
- String-char array
- String-object
- Short

Arduino Function Libraries

- **Input/ Output Functions:**
    - The Arduino pins can be configured to act as input or output pins using the pinMode() function

```
Void setup ()
{
pinMode(pin , mode);
}
```
Pin-pin number on the Arduinoboard
Mode-INPUT/OUTPUT

- **digitalWrite()** : It used to writes a HIGH or LOW value to a digital pin
- **analogRead()** : Reads from the analog input pin i.e., voltage applied across the pin
- Character functions such as **isdigit(),isspace()**, **isalpha(),islower()**, **isalnum()**, **isxdigit(),isupper()**,return 1(true) or 0(false)
- **Delay()** function is used to provide a delay of specified time. It accepts integer value (time in miliseconds). It is one of the most common time manipulation function.

Operators in Arduino

- Arithmetic Operators: =, +, -, *, /, %
- Boolean Operator: &&, ||, !
- Comparison Operator: ==, !=, <, >, <=, >=
- Bitwise Operator: &, |, ^, ~, <<, >>,
- Compound Operator: ++, --, +=, -=, *=, /=, %=, |=, &=

Control Statement

If statement
```
if(condition){
Statements if the
condition is true ;
}
```
If...Else statement
```
if(condition ){
Statements if the
condition is true;
}
else{
Statements if the
condition is false;
}
```
If.......Elseif.....Else
```
if (condition1){
Statements if the
condition1 is true;
}
else if (condition2){
Statements if the
condition1 is false
and condition2 is true; }
```

else{
Statements if both the
conditions are false;
}

Switch Case

Switch(choice)
{
case opt1: statement_1;break;
case opt2: statement_2;break;
case opt3: statement_3;break;
.
.
.
case default: statement_default; break;
}

Conditional Operator

Val=(condition)?(Statement1): (Statement2)

Loops

For loop

for(initialization; condition; increment){
Statement till the condition is true;
}

While loop

while(condition){
Statement till the condition is true;
}

Do... While loop

do{
Statement till the condition is true;
}while(condition);

Nested loop

Calling a loop inside another loop

Infinite loop

Condition of the loop is always true, the loop will never terminate.

Arrays

- Collection of elements having homogenous data type that are stored in adjacent memory location.
- The conventional starting index is 0.
- Declaration of array:
  <Datatype>array_name[size];
  Ex: intarre[5];

Multi-dimensional array Declaration:

<Datatype>array_name[n1] [n2][n3]....;

Ex: intarre[row][col][height];

String

- Array of characters with NULL as termination is termed as a String.
- Declaration using Array:
    o char str[]="ABCD";
    o char str[4];
        ▪ str[0]='A';
        ▪ str[0]='B';
        ▪ str[0]='C';
        ▪ str[0]=0;
- Declaration using String Object:
    o String str="ABC";

Functions of String Object

- str.ToUpperCase()
- str.replace(str1,str2)
- str.length()

Math Library

Math library is used to apply the math functions and mathematical constants, by using "MATH.h" header files.

Functions:

- cos(double radian);
- sin(double radian);
- tan(double radian);
- fabs(double val);
- fmod(double val1, double val2);

Functions:

- exp(double val);
- log(double val);
- log10(double val);
- square(double val);
- pow(double base, double power);

Random Number

- randomSeed(intv): reset the pseudo-random number generator with seed value v
- random(maxi)=gives a random number within the range [0,maxi]
- random(mini,maxi)=gives a random number within the range [mini,maxi]

Interrupts

- An external signal for which system blocks the current running process to process that signal

Types of interrupt:

    o Hardware interrupt
    o Software interrupt

- digitalPinToInterrupt(pin): Change actual digital pin to the specific interrupt number.

27

- attachInterrupt(digitalPinToInterrupt(pin), ISR, mode);
  - ○ ISR: a interrupt service routine have to be defined.

Sensors

- Sensors are Electronic elements.
- It converts physical quantity/ measurements into electrical signals.
- It can be analog or digital.

Types of Sensors

Some commonly used sensors are as follows:

- Temperature
- Compass
- Humidity
- Light
- Accelerometer
- Sound

Actuators

- Actuators is a Mechanical/Electro-mechanical device.
- It used to converts energy into motion.
- Actuators are mainly used to provide controlled motion to other components.

Types of Motor Actuators

- Servo motor
- Stepper motor
- Solenoid
- Hydraulic motor
- AC motor
- Relay

Servo Motor

- Servo Motor is a high precision motor
- It provides rotary motion 0 to 180 degree
- There are 3 wires in the Servo motor
- The Black or the darkest one is Ground
- Another one is red for power supply
- The Yellow for signal pin

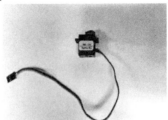

Fig: Servo Motor

Servo Library on Arduino
- Arduinoprovides different library-SERVO to operate the servo motor
- Create an instance of servo to use it in the sketch

Servo myservo;

Sketch: SERVO_ACTUATOR

```
#include <Servo.h>
//Including the servo library for the program
intservoPin = 12;

Servo ServoDemo; // Creating a servo object
void setup() {
// The servo pin must be attached to the servo
before it can be used
ServoDemo.attach(servoPin);
}

voidloop(){
//Servomovesto0 degrees
ServoDemo.write(0);
delay(1000);

//Servomovesto90 degrees
ServoDemo.write(90);
delay(1000);

// Servomovesto180 degrees
ServoDemo.write(180);
delay(1000);
}
```

Python
- Python is a versatile language
- It can be script and read easily.
- It doesn't support strict rules for syntax.
- Its installation comes with integrated development environment for programming.
- It supports interfacing with wide ranging hardware platforms.
- With open-source nature, it forms a strong backbone to build large applications.

Python IDE
- Python IDE is a free and open source software
- It is used to write codes, integrate several modules and libraries.
- It is available for installation into PC with Windows, Linux and Mac.
- Examples: Spyder, PyCharm, etc.

Starting with Python

It is simple printing statement at the python interpreter prompt,

```
>>> print "Hi!"
```
Output: Hi!

The following code indicate different blocks of code.

```
if True:
        print "Correct"
else:
        print "Error"
```

Data-types in Python
There are 5 data types in Python:
- Numbers
- String
- List
- Tuple
- Dictionary

Numbers
Numbers x, y, z = 1, 2.2, " IoT"

String
```
x = 'This is Python'
print x              >>This is Python
print x[0]           >>T
print x[2:4]         >>is
```

List
List x = [1, 2.2, 'IoT']

Dictionary
d = {1:'item','k':2}

Controlling Statements
- **if**

```
if (cond.):
        statement 1
        statement 2
elif(cond.):
        statement 1
        statement 2
else:
        statement 1
        statement 2
```

- **while**

```
while (cond.):
        statement 1
        statement 2
```

- x = [1,2,3,4]

```
foriin x:
        statement 1
        statement 2
```

- **Break**

```
for s in "string":
        if s == 'n':
                break
        print (s)
print "End"
```

- **Continue**

```
for s in "string":
        if s == 'y':
                continue
        print (s)
print "End"
```

Functions in Python

Defining a function

- **Without return value**

```
deffunct_name(arg1, arg2, arg3):        # Defining the function
        statement 1
        statement 2
```

- **With return value**

```
deffunct_name(arg1, arg2, arg3):        # Defining the function
        statement 1
        statement 2
        return x                        # Returning the value
```

- **Calling a function**

```
defexample (str):
        print (str+ "!")
example ("Hello")                       # Calling the function
Output: Hello!
```

Variable Scope in Python

Global variables

These are the variables declared out of any function, but can be accessed inside as well as outside the function.

Local variables

These are the ones that are declared inside a function.

```
Example showing Global Variable
g_var= 10
defexample():
l_var= 100
print(g_var)
example()                               # calling the function
```

```
Output:: 10
Example showing Variable Scope
var= 10
defexample():
var= 100
print(var)
example()                               # calling the function print(var)
```

Output:: 100 10

Modules in Python

- Any segment of code fulfilling a particular task that can be used commonly by everyone is termed as a module.

Syntax:

importmodule_name   #At the top of the code

usingmodule_name.var   #To access functions and values with 'var' in the module

Example:

import random
foriin range(1,10):
        val= random.randint(1,10)
        print (val)

Output:: varies with each execution

- We can also access only a particular function from a module.

Example:

from math import pi
print (pi)

Output:: 3.14159

Exception Handling in Python

- An error that is generated during execution of a program, is termed as exception.

Syntax:

try:
        statements
except _Exception_:
        statements
else:
        statements

Example:

while True:
        try:
                n = input ("Please enter an integer: ")
                n = int(n)
                break
        exceptValueError:
                print "No valid integer! "
print "It is an integer!"

File Read Write Operations

- Python allows you to read and write files
- No separate module or library required

32

- Three basic steps
  - Open a file
  - Read/Write
  - Close the file

Opening a File:
- Open() function is used to open a file, returns a file object
- open(file_name, mode)

Mode:
Four basic modes to open a file
- r: read mode
- w: write mode
- a: append mode
- r+: both read and write mode

Read from a file:
- read(): Reads from a file
  file=open('data.txt', 'r')
  file.read()

Write to a file:
- Write(): Writes to a file
  file=open('data.txt', 'w')
  file.write('writing to the file')

Closing a file:
- Close(): This is done to ensure that the file is free to use for other resources file.close()

Networking in Python
- Python provides network services for client server model.
- Socket support in the operating system allows to implement clients and servers for both connection-oriented and connectionless protocols.
- Python has libraries that provide higher-level access to specific application-level network protocols.

Syntax for creating a socket:
  s = socket.socket (socket_family, socket_type, protocol=0)
socket_family– AF_UNIX or AF_INET
socket_type– SOCK_STREAM or SOCK_DGRAM
protocol– default '0'.

Raspberry Pi
- It means the computer in your palm.
- It is Single-board computer.
- It is cost effective and it ca be accessed easily.

Specifications

Key features	Raspberry pi 3 model B	Raspberry pi 2 model B	Raspberry Pi zero
RAM	1GB SDRAM	1GB SDRAM	512 MB SDRAM
CPU	Quad cortex A53@1.2GHz	Quad cortex A53@900MHz	ARM 11@ 1GHz
GPU	400 MHz video core IV	250 MHz video core IV	250 MHz video core IV
Ethernet	10/100	10/100	None
Wireless	802.11/Bluetooth 4.0	None	None
Video output	HDMI/Composite	HDMI/Composite	HDMI/Composite
GPIO	40	40	40

Basic Architecture

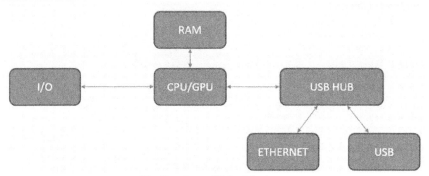

Fig. Raspberry Pi Architecture

Fig. Raspberry Pi

34

Operating System
- Official Supported OS :
- Raspbian
- NOOBS

Some of the third party OS :
- UBUNTU mate
- Windows 10 core
- Risc OS
- Snappy Ubuntu core
- Pinet

Applications of Raspberry Pi
- Media streamer
- Home automation
- VPN
- Tablet computer
- Controlling BOT
- Light weight web server for IOT

SDN –Recap

- **SDN-Software-Defined Networking**
- SDN –restructuring current network infrastructure
- Architecture of SDN –Application, Control and Infrastructure layers
- Rule Placement –TCAM and Delay
- OpenFlow protocol –flow-rule and math-fields

APIs in SDN

- **Southbound API**
  - The communication takes place between control layer and infrastructure layer.
  - Here openFlow protocol is used.
- **Northbound API**
  - It used to communicate between control layer and application layer.
  - Standard APIs are used.
- **East-Westbound APIs**
  - Used to communicate among multiple controllers in the control layer.

Flat Architecture

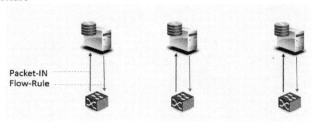

Hierarchical (tree) Architecture

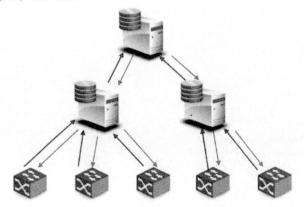

Ring Architecture

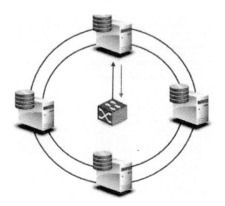

Mesh Architecture

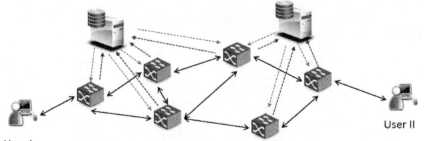

Internet of Things

- It is an Creating an interactive environment
- Network of devices connected togetherIoT Applications

Remote Data Logging

- **Remote Data Logging**used to collect data from the devices in the network
- The data can be send to a server/remote machine
- Later the data can be processed.
- Finally it is respond to the network

System Overview:

- A network of Temperature and humidity sensor connected with Raspberry Pi
- Read data from the sensor and send it to a Server
- The data can be saved in the server
- Data Splitting
- Plot the data

Requirements

- DHT Sensor
- Jumper wires
- 4.7K ohm resistor
- Raspberry Pi

DHT Sensor

- Digital Humidity and Temperature Sensor (DHT)
- PIN 1, 2, 3, 4 (from left to right)
- PIN 1-3.3V-5V Power supply
- PIN 2-Data
- PIN 3-Null
- PIN 4-Ground

Fig: DHT Sensor

Sensor-Raspberry Pi Interface

- DHT sensor 1st pin is connected to the 3.3V pin of Raspberry Pi
- DHT sensor 2nd pin is connect to any input pins of Raspberry Pi, here we have used pin 11
- DHT sensor 4th pin is connected to the ground pin of the Raspberry Pi

Fig: Sensor-Raspberry Pi Interface

Read Data from the Sensor

- Use the Adafruitlibrary for DHT22 sensor to read the sensor data

 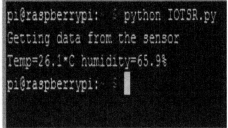

Sending Data to a Server

- Using socket programming data is send to server
- Create a client and server
- Establish connection between the client and server

- The data can be send from the client to the server
- Save the data in a file

Data Processing

Data from the client needs to be processed before it can be used further
- Data splitting/filtering
- Data plotting

Data Processing
- Data splitting/filtering:
- Data from the client is saved in a text file
- The values are separated by a comma(' , ')

message = str(h)+','+str(t)

- Split() function can be used to split a string into multiple strings depending on the type of separator/delimiter specified.

Example:
- Data= 'sunday,monday,tuesday'   #Data is a string with 3 words separated by a comma
- Data.split(",")   # split the data whenever a "," is found
- ['sunday','monday','tuesday']   # Gives 3 different strings as output

Plotting the data:

MATPLOTLIB is a python library used to plot in 2D
- Plot(x,y): plots the values x and y
- xlabel('X Axis'): Labels the x-axis
- ylabel('Y Axis'): Labels the y-axis
- title("Simple Plot"): Adds title to the plot

Plotting the data:
- import matplotlib.pyplotas
- myplotmyplot.plot([1,2,3,4])
- myplot.ylabel('Y-Axis')
- myplot.show()

- By default the values are taken for y-axis, values for x-axis are generated automatically starting from 0

Basic Plot

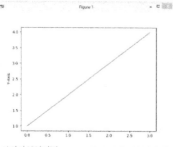

```
import matplotlib.pyplot as myplot
myplot.plot([ , , , ])
myplot.ylabel("Y Axis")
myplot.show()
```

Some other common functions used in plotting:
- figure(): Creates a new figure
- grid(): Enable or disable axis grids in the plot
- Scatter(): make a scatter plot of the given points
- ion(): turns on the interactive mode
- Close(): Close the current figure window
- subplot(): Adds subplot in a figure

Sending Data to a Server

Client:
```
defsensordata():
GPIO.setmode(GPIO.BOARD)
GPIO.setwarnings(False)
sensor = Adafruit_DHT.AM2302
humidity, temperature = Adafruit_DHT.read_retry(sensor,17) return(humidity, temperature)
sock = socket.socket(socket.AF_INET, socket.SOCK_DGRAM) #create UDP socket
server_address= ('10.14.3.194', 10001)
try:
while (1):
h,t= sensordata()
message = str(h)+','+str(t) #Send data
print>>sys.stderr, 'sending "%s"' % message
sent = sock.sendto(message, server_address)
finally:
print>>sys.stderr, 'closing socket'
sock.close()
```

Server:
```
defcoverage_plot(data,i):
hum=data.split(",")[0]
tem=data.split(",")[1]
print 'temp='+(str(tem))+'iter='+str(i)
plt.ion()
fig=plt.figure(num=1,figsize=(6,6))
plt.title(' IoTTemperature and Humidity Monitor')
ax= fig.add_subplot(121)
ax.plot(tem,i, c='r', marker=r'$\Theta$')
plt.xlabel('Temp ($^0 C$)')
ax.grid()
ax= fig.add_subplot(122)
ax.plot(hum,i, c='b', marker=r'$\Phi$')
plt.xlabel('Humidity ($\%$)')
ax.grid()
fig.show()
fig.canvas.draw()
```

```
sock = socket.socket(socket.AF_INET, socket.SOCK_DGRAM)
# Bind the socket to the port
server_address= ('10.14.3.194', 10001)
sock.bind(server_address)
i=0
while True:
data, address = sock.recvfrom(4096)
with open("DataLog.txt","a") as f:
mess=str(data)
f.write(mess) \coverage_plot(mess,i)
print mess i+=1
f.close()
```
Output
- The Reading from the sensor is sent to the Server and saved in a text file.
- Two different plots for temperature and humidity data

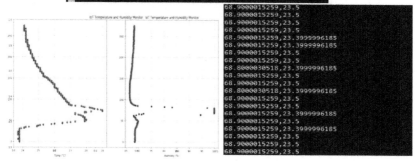

IoT Architecture

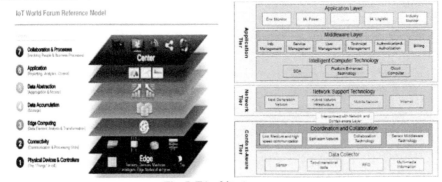

Fig: IoTArchitecture

Benefits of Integrating SDN in IoT

- Intelligent routing decisions can be deployed using SDN
- Simplification of information collection, analysis and decision making
- Visibility of network resources –network management is simplified based on user, device and application-specific requirements
- Intelligent traffic pattern analysis and coordinated decisions

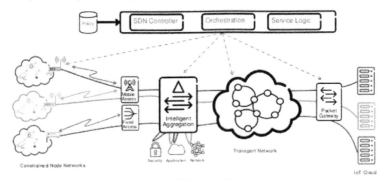

Fig: SDN for IoT-I

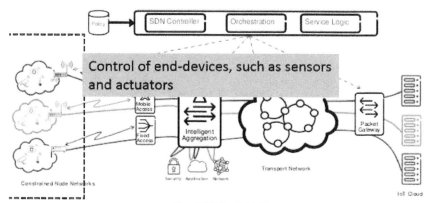

Fig: SDN for IoT-II

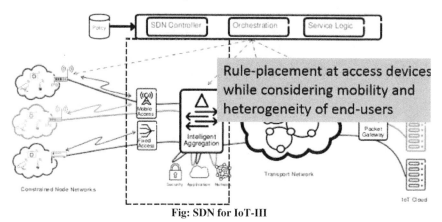

Fig: SDN for IoT-III

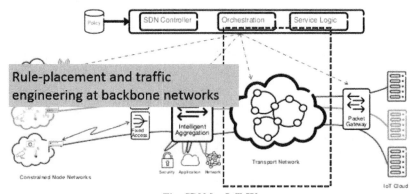

Fig: SDN for IoT-IV

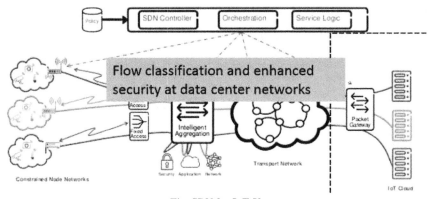

Fig: SDN for IoT-V

SDN for IoT-Recap

- Software-Defined WSN
- Different approaches –Sensor OpenFlow, Soft-WSN, SDNWISE
- Software-Defined WSN can improve overall performance over traditional WSN

Problems in Traditional Mobile Network

- Difficult to Scale
- Difficult to manage
- Inflexible
- Cost-expensive

SDN for Mobile Networking I

Flow-Table Paradigm of SDN

- Well suited for end-to-end communication over multiple technologies such as WiFi, 3G, 4G, etc.

Logically Centralized Control

- Particularly useful for efficient base-station coordination for addressing inter-cell interference

Path Management

- Data can be routed based on service requirements without depending on core routing policies

Network Virtualization

- Abstracts the physical resources from the network services
- Helps in providing seamless connectivity and service differentiation among users

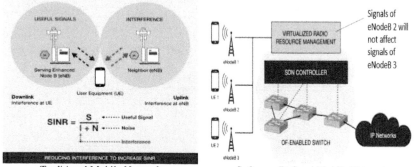

Traditional Mobile Network   Software-Defined Mobile Network

SDWMN-Use Case: Mobile Traffic Management

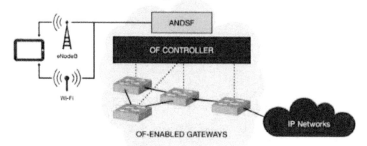

- Mobile traffic offloading based on Open Flow
- ANDSF –access network discovery and service function

Key Benefits

- Centralized control of devices manufactured by multiple vendors
- Higher rate of integration of new services

45

- Abstracted network control and management
- Network abstracted from the user

Approaches
- ODIN
- Ubi-Flow
- Mobi-Flow

ODIN-I

An agent is placed at access points to communicate with controller
Two components are present
- Odin agent –placed with the physical devices
- Odin master –placed at the controller end

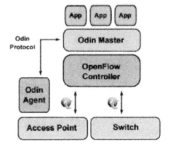

Fig: ODIN-I

ODIN-II
- Conversion of 802.11
- LVAP –Light virtual AP

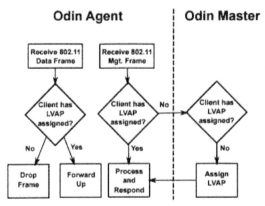

Fig: ODIN-II

Ubi-Flow I

46

Mobility management in SDIoT
- Scalable control of the APs
- Fault tolerance

Flow-Scheduling
- Network partition
- Network matching
- Load balancing

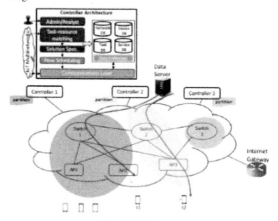

Fig: Ubi-Flow I

Mobi-Flow I
Mobility-aware flow-rule placement in SDIoT

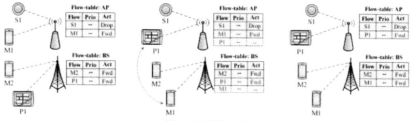

Fig: Mobi-Flow I

Mobi-Flow II
- Proactive rule placement depending on users' movement in the network

Approach
- Predict location of end-users at (t+1) time, while the users are at (t) time
- Place flow-rules at the APs which can be associated to the users based on their predicted locations.

Mobi-Flow III

47

Location prediction
- Order-K Markov predictor –takes last k-thlocation instances to predict next location

Flow-rule placement
- Linear programming can be used to select optimal AP

Mobi-Flow IV

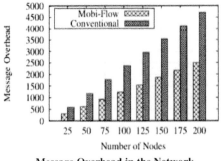

Message Overhead in the Network

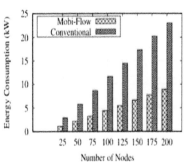

Energy consumption in the Network

Control message overhead and energy consumption can be minimized significantly using Mobi-Flow compared to the conventional flow-rule placement schemes.

Data Center Networking
- Mice-Flow –Wildcard rules can be placed to deal with miceflows
- Elephant Flow –Exact match rules are useful

Recent Trends in Computing

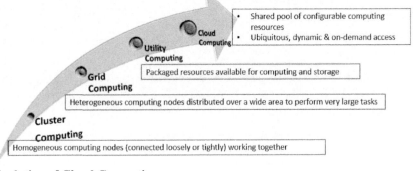

Evolution of Cloud Computing

48

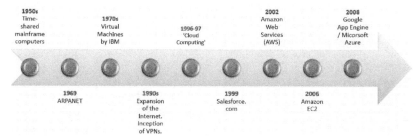

Cloud computing

"Cloud computing is a model for enabling convenient, on-demand network access to a shared pool of configurable computing resources (e.g., network infrastructures, servers,storage,applications,etc.)"–NIST

- It can be envisioned as step on from Utility Computing
- It provides high level generalization (abstraction) of computation and storage model
- It can be rapidly allocated and released with low management effort
- It has some essential characteristics, service models, and deployment models
- It provides on-demand services, which can be accessed from any place and at anytime.

NIST Visual Model of Cloud Computing

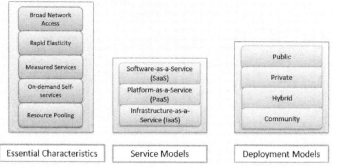

Business Advantages

- Nearly zero cost for upfront infrastructure investment
- Real-time Infrastructure availability
- More efficient resource utilization
- Usage-based costing
- Reduced time to market

General Characteristics

- Improved agilityin resource provisioning.
- Ubiquitous–independent of device or location
- Multitenancy–sharing of resources and costs across a large pool of users

- Dynamic load balancing
- Highly reliableand scalable
- Low cost and low maintenance
- Improved security and access control

Essential Characteristics
- Broad network access
- Rapid elasticity
- Measured service
- On-demand self-service
- Resource pooling

Components of Cloud Computing
- Clients /end-users:Thick, Thin, Mobile
- Services:Products& solutions (Identity, Mapping, Search, etc.)
- Applications:Web apps, SaaS, etc.
- Platform:Apps/Web hosting using PaaS
- Storage:Database, Data-Storage-as-a-Service (DSaaS)
- Infrastructure:Virtualization, IaaS, EC2

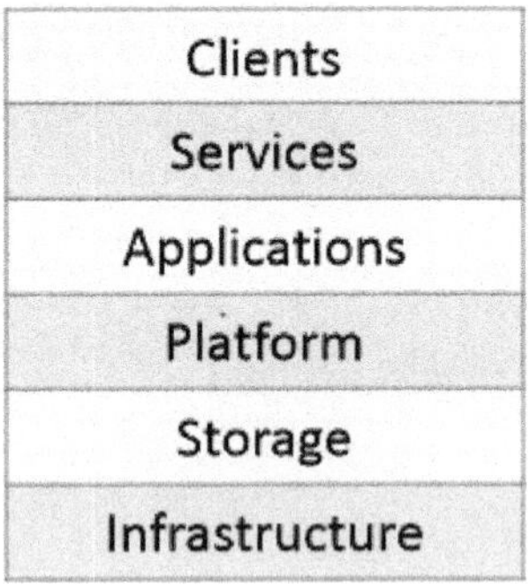

Clients
Services
Applications
Platform
Storage
Infrastructure

Service Models
- Software-as-a-Service (SaaS)
- Platform-as-a-Service (PaaS)
- Infrastructure-as-a-Service (IaaS)

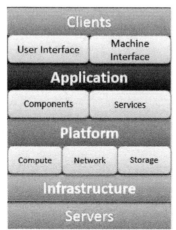

Software-as-a-Service (SaaS)
- Facility to execute service provider's applications at user's end
- Applications are available as 'services'
- Services can be accessed via different types of client devices (e.g. web browser, app)
- End-users do not possess the control of the cloud infrastructure

Examples:
> Google Apps
> Salesforce
> Learn.com.

Platform-as-a-Service (PaaS)
- Facility for the consumer to execute consumer-createdor acquired applicationsonto cloud infrastructure
- Support for deployment of such applications
- The user does not control the cloud infrastructure
- User can control the deployed applications using given configurations

Examples:
> Windows Azure
> Google AppEngine

Infrastructure-as-a-Service (IaaS)
- Facility to access computing resources such as network, storage, and operating system
- User can deploy, execute and control any software (Operating systemsand other applications)
- In some case, the user can control selected networking components (e.g., host firewalls).

Examples:
> Amazon EC2
> GoGrid
> Iland

Rackspace Cloud Servers.

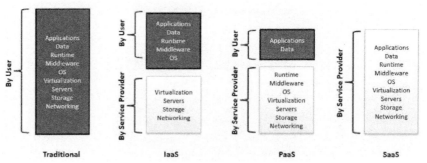

Fig: Comparison of Different Service Models

Deployment Models
Public cloud
Private cloud
Hybrid cloud
Others:
Distributed cloud
Inter-cloud
Community cloud
Multi-cloud

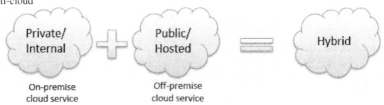

Off-premise
cloud service

On-premise
cloud service

Fig: Deployment Models

Public Cloud
• Cloud set-up for the use of any person or industry
• Typically owned by an organization who offers the cloud service.
Examples:
  Amazon Web Service (AWS)
  Google Compute Engine
  Microsoft Azure

Advantages:
• Easy to set-up at low cost, as provider covers the hardware, application and bandwidth costs.
• Scalability to meet needs.
• Pay-per-use ensures that from user's perspective no resources wasted.

Private Cloud

- Cloud set-up functioned only for a single organization
- Typically managed by the organization itself (on-premises) or a third party (off-premises)

Advantages:
Total control over the system and data
Minimum security concerns

Disadvantages:
Regular maintenance

	Public Cloud	Private Cloud
Virtualized resources	Publicly shared	Privately shared
Customer types	Multiple	Limited
Connectivity	Over Internet	Over Internet/private network
Security	Low	High

Fig: Public Cloud vs Private Cloud

Hybrid Cloud
- Cloud set-up constructed by two or more unique cloud set-up (private, community, or public)
- Pooled together by standardized tools
- Supports data and application portability (e.g., facility for load-balancing between clouds)
- Provides multiple deployment models

Other Types of Cloud

Distributed Cloud
- Collection of scattered set of computing devices in different locations, however, connected to a single network
- Two types –
  - Public-resource Computing
  - Volunteer Cloud.

Inter-cloud
- Unified global 'cloud of clouds 'based on the Internet
- Supports interoperability between cloud service providers

Community cloud
- Shared set-up between several organizations having common concerns (security, compliance, jurisdiction, etc.)
- Managed by internally or by third party.

Multi-cloud
- Multiple cloud computing services offered via single heterogeneous architecture
- Increases fault-tolerance and flexibility.

	On-premise	Off-premise
Dedicated Access	Private cloud	Hosted private cloud
Shared Access	Community cloud	Public cloud

Introduction to Openstack

- A software to create a cloud unfrastructure
- Launched as a joint project of Rackspace Hosting and NASA in 2010
- Open source
- Presently many companies are contributing to openstackEg. IBM, CISCO, HP, Dell, Vmware , Redhat, suse, Rackspace hosting
- It has a very large community
- Can be used to develop private cloud or public cloud
- Versions:

Austin, Bexar, Cactus, Diablo, Essex, Folsom, Grizzly, Havana, Icehouse, Juno, Kilo, Liberty, Mitaka, Newton, Ocata(Latest)

Fig:Components

Components

Keystone

- Identity service
- Provides authentication and authorization

Horizon

- Dashboard
- GUI of the software
- Provides overview of the other components

Nova

- Compute service
- Where you launce your instances

Glance

- Image service

54

- Discovering, registering, retrieving the VM
- Snapshots

Swift
- Object storage
- Helps in storing data safely, cheaply and efficiently

Neutron
- Provides networking service
- Enables the other services to communicate with each other
- Make your own network

Cinder
- Block storage
- Virtualizes the management of block service

Heat
- Orchestration

Ceilometer
- Billing
- What service you are using
- How long are you using

Smart City

- A Smart City is an urban system and uses Information & Communication Technology (ICT)
- It makes the infrastructure more interactive, accessible and efficient.

Need for Smart Cities -

- Rapidly growing urban population
- Fast depleting natural resources
- Changes in environment and climate

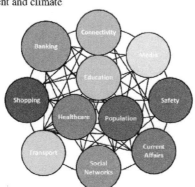

Fig:Smart People

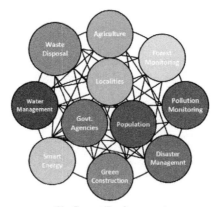

Fig:Smart Environment

Current Focus Areas

Smart Homes

- Health monitoring.
- Conservation of resources (e.g. electricity, water, fuel).
- Security and safety.

Smart Parking Lots

- Auto routing of vehicles to empty slots.
- Auto charging for services provided.
- Detection of vacant slots in the parking lot.

Smart Vehicles

- Assistance to drivers during bad weather or low-visibility.
- Detection of bad driving patterns or driving under the influence of substances.
- Auto alert generation during crashes.
- Self-diagnostics.

Smart Health

- Low cost, portable, at-home medical diagnosis kits.
- Remote check-ups and diagnosis.
- On-body sensors for effortless and accurate health monitoring.
- Auto alert generation in case of emergency medical episodes (e.g. Heart attacks, seizures).

Pollution and Calamity Monitoring

- Monitoring for weather or man-made based calamities.
- Alert generation in case of above-threshold pollutants in the air or water.
- Resource reallocation and rerouting of services in the event of calamities.

Smart Energy

- Smart metering systems.
- Smart energy allocation and distribution system.
- Incorporation of traditional and renewable sources of energy in the same grid.

56

Smart Agriculture

- Automatic detection of plant water stress.
- Monitoring of crop health status.
- Auto detection of crop infection.
- Auto application of fertilizers and pesticides.
- Scheduling harvesting and arranging proper transfer of harvests to warehouses or markets.

IoT Challenges in Smart Cities

- ✓ Security and Privacy
- ✓ Heterogeneity
- ✓ Reliability
- ✓ Large scale
- ✓ Legal and Social aspects
- ✓ Big data
- ✓ Sensor Networks

Table of Contents

Printed in Great Britain
by Amazon

66033774R00041